# IN FOCUS

# POLAR LANDS

# KINGFISHER

First published 2017 by Kingfisher
an imprint of Macmillan Children's Books
20 New Wharf Road, London N1 9RR
Associated companies throughout the world
www.panmacmillan.com

Series editor: Hayley Down
Design: Jeni Child

ISBN 978-0-7534-4107-7

9 8 7 6 5 4 3 2 1

1TR/0417/WKT/UG/128MA

A CIP catalogue record for this book is available from the British Library.

Printed in China

Picture credits
The Publisher would like to thank the following for permission to reproduce their material.
Top = t; Bottom = b; Middle = m; Left = l; Right = r
Front cover: Getty/Wayne Lynch; Back cover: Shutterstock/Mikael Broms; Cover flap: iStock/KeithSzafranski; Page 1 iStock/carlaexmota; 3 iStock/Grafissimo;
4–5 iStock/Terraxplorer; 4t Shutterstock/Sara Winter; 4b iStock/KenCanning; 5 iStock/kovalchuk; 6 iStock/Terraxplorer; 7t Alamy/blickwinkel; 7m Getty/Hiroya
Minakuchi; 7b Alamy/ton koene; 8–9 Shutterstock/Mikael Broms; 10tl Getty/UniversalImagesGroup; 10m Shutterstock; 10b Shutterstock/Avatar_023; 11tm
Shutterstock/Pavel Svoboday; 11tr Getty/UniversalImageGroup; 11b Shutterstock/2j architecture; 12 Getty/Bettman; 13t Alamy/Archive Pics; 13m Getty/Bettman;
13b Getty/Bob Haswell; 14b Creative Commons; 15t Alamy/blickwinkel; 15b Alamy/REUTERS; 16–17 iStock/sodar99; 18t Getty/Alasdair Turner; 18bl NASA;
18br Getty/Paul Nicken; 19tGetty/Dymtryo Pylypenko; 19bl Getty Paul Nicken; 19brGetty/Carsten Peter; 20–21 Shutterstock/Dymtryo Pylypenko; 21t iStock/
encrier; 22–23 Alamy/Steve Bloom Images; 24 (1) 25tl (2) Alamy/Charlie Summers; 25tl (3) Alamy/Paul Souders; 25ml (4)Shutterstock/Mogens Trolle; 25bl (5)
Shutterstock/JoCrebbin; 25bl (6) Shutterstock/Anders Peter Photography; 25tr (7) Alamy/KeithSzafranski; 25tr (8) Shutterstock/Natural Earth Imagery; 25mr (9)
Shutterstock/Anton_Ivanov; 25br (10) Alamy/Andrew Walmsley; 26–27t Shutterstock/Volodymyr Kyrylyuk; 26tl Alamy/age fotostock; 26tr Alamy/Ilukee; 26bl
Shutterstock/Nicram Sabod; 26br iStock/4loops; 27bl Alamy/Steven J. Kazlowski; 28–29 Alamy/blickwinkel; 30 (1) Shutterstock/
JoCrebbin; 31tl (2) iStock/Lazareva; 31tl (3) Shutterstock/Geoffrey Kuchera; 31ml (4) iStock/LeFion; 31bl (5)Getty/Paul Nicklen; 31bl (6) iStock/KenCanning; 31tr
(7) iStock/FRANKHILDEBRAND; 31tr (8) iStock/pilipenkoD; 31mr (9) iStock/Robjem; 31br (10) iStock/richLindie; 32t iStock/SeventhDayPhotography; 32b iStock/
mzphoto11; 33t iStock/mzphoto11; 33m iStock/mikeuk; 33b iStock/zanskar; 34–35 Alamy/blickwinkel; 36–37 Alamy/Paul Souders; 37r Alamy/Paulette Sinclair;
38 (1) Shutterstock/Boris Pamikov; 39tl (2) Getty/Paul Nicklen; 39tl (3) iStock/oceanbounddb; 39ml (4) Alamy/blickwinkel; 39bl (5) Alamy/WILDLIFE GmbH; 39bl
(6) Alamy/cbimages; 39tr (7) Creative Commons; 39tr (8) Alamy/Norbert Wu; 39mr (9) Alamy/Accent Alaska; 39br (10) Nature PL; 40 Getty/wildestanimal; 41t
Alamy/WaterFrame; 41b iStock/PaulWolf; 42–43 Alamy/blickwinkel; 44 iStock/kovalchuk; 45t iStock/Icarmen13; 45m iStock/IPGGutenbergUKLtd; 45b iStock/
MichaelVacchiano; 46–47 Shutterstock/Kirk Geisler; 48 (1) Getty/Time Life Pictures; 49tl (2) Shutterstock/IgorGolovniov; 49tl (3) Getty/CANOVAS Alvaro; 49ml
(4) Alamy/ZUMA Press; 49bl (5) Getty/ Scott Polar Research Institue, University of Cambridge; 49bl (6) Getty/Bettman; 49tr (7) Getty/Gordon Wiltsie; 49tr
(8) Creative Commons; 49mr (9) Creative Commons; 49br (10) Getty/LEON NEAL; 50t Creative Commons; 50b Shutterstock/Evgeny Kovalev spb; 51t Creative
Commons; 51b Creative Commons; 52–53 (1) Tom McShane Photography; 52br (2)Creative Commons; 52br (3) Creative Commons; 53bl (4) Red Bull; 53bl (5)
Creative Commons; 53r (6)Alamy/William Sutton; 53mr (7) iStock; 53mr (8) AGCO Corp; 53br (9) Getty/Mike Flokis; 53br (10) iStock/Laszlo Szirtesi; 54–55 iStock/
SeppFriedhuber; 56t Alamy/robertharding; 56m Getty/Universal History Archive; 57t Shutterstock/Anton_Ivanov; 57m Alamy/John Frost Newspapers; 58 Getty/
Galen Rowell; 59t Alamy/Stocktrek Images, Inc.; 59b Alamy/Radharc Images; 60 Shutterstock/Denis Burdin; 61 iStock/KeithSzafranski; 62–63 iStock.

# IN FOCUS

# POLAR LANDS

### BY CLIVE GIFFORD

KINGFISHER

# CONTENTS

# WELCOME TO THE
# ENDS OF THE EARTH!

The extreme north and south of the planet are known as the North Pole and the South Pole. The land and waters around each pole make up the **polar** regions. In the south is icy Antarctica; in the north, a mixture of Arctic Ocean, ice sheets and parts of North America, Europe and Asia.

The polar regions have much in common. The Sun never sets during their summers, and their winters bring bitterly cold temperatures. Yet, despite the hostile conditions, both are home to some incredible creatures and stunning sights!

snow-capped mountains
in northern Norway

# INSIDE YOU'LL FIND ...

... blue icebergs

**EXPERIENCE** the geography and climate at the poles and their extraordinary scenery and features, from dazzling light shows to icebergs bigger than whole countries!

... awesome animals

**FROZEN FACT**

**CHECK OUT** seals, penguins, polar bears and lots, lots more fascinating creatures that make the freezing polar regions their home.

... polar people

**FROZEN FACT**

**LEARN ABOUT** the brave and resourceful people who live in, work in and explore the polar regions.

# POLAR WORLD

# NORTH VERSUS

**NORTH:** We think of the Arctic as all the land and sea that lies within the Arctic Circle. The North Pole is found in the middle of the Arctic Ocean.

## NORTH FACT FILE

**Highest point:** Mount Gunnbjörn, Greenland (3694 m)
**Nearest ocean:** Arctic Ocean
**Midsummer:** 21 June
**Midwinter:** 21 December
**Highest temperature at North Pole:** 5 °C
**Lowest temperature at North Pole:** −43 °C
**Permanent population:** 4 million
**Biggest settlement:** Murmansk, Russia (approx. 307,000 people)

## ARCTIC PEOPLE

People have lived within the **Arctic Circle** for thousands of years. Many live **nomadic** lives, moving from place to place hunting and sometimes herding animals. Oil, fishing, mining and trading have prompted the founding of some towns in the Arctic, including Murmansk in Russia and Tromsø in Norway.

**FROZEN FACT** **TEMPERATURES** lower than −40 °C are common in winter in the Russian Arctic town of Oymyakon. Schoolkids there have to be tough. The school gained its first indoor toilet in 2008 and school only closes if the temperature plummets to −52 °C!

reindeer

# SOUTH

**SOUTH:** The Antarctic includes islands, parts of the Southern Ocean and the continent of Antarctica. The South Pole is in the middle of Antarctica.

## SOUTH FACT FILE

**Highest point:** Mount Vinson (4892 m)
**Nearest ocean:** Southern Ocean
**Midsummer:** 21 December
**Midwinter:** 21 June
**Highest temperature at South Pole:** −13.5 °C
**Lowest temperature at South Pole:** −82.8 °C
**Permanent population:** 0
**Biggest settlement:** McMurdo Station (approx. 1200 people)

## ANTARCTIC PEOPLES

No one lives permanently in Antarctica but around 4000–5000 visitors live and work at bases and science stations on the **continent** during the summer. This number drops to around 1000 in winter. In the summer, about 40,000 tourists visit, mostly by ships for short trips.

**FROZEN FACT** The **COLDEST** temperature ever recorded on the Earth was at the Vostok Research Station in Antarctica in 1983. It was a bone-chilling, teeth-chattering −89.2 °C – four times colder than a household freezer!

penguins

# REACHING THE NORTH POLE

The North Pole can be a confusing place. When people say they have reached it on land, they really mean they are floating above it, on large pieces of ice. And when they have tried to mark the Pole's place by placing a flag or sign, they find that, as the shifting sea ice moves, their marker eventually drifts away!

## More than one Pole

Did you know there's more than one North Pole? There is the magnetic North Pole, which is the place the needle on a compass points to when it indicates north. This is around 500 kilometres away from the geographic North Pole, the most northerly point of the planet. Will Steger reached the North Pole by dog sled in 1986.

**Will Steger**

Robert Peary

history mystery

No one is certain who reached the **NORTH POLE** first. Maybe ancient Arctic people, such as the Inuit, or one of the explorers who claimed to reach it in the early 20th century, such as Frederick Cook or Robert Peary.

FROZEN FACT

The first successful flight over the North Pole was by the airship **NORGE** in 1926. It contained famous explorer Roald Amundsen. In 1949, two men parachuted down to the Pole for the first time – awesome!

fly over

NI NORGE

underwater exploring

FROZEN FACT

In 1958, the **USS NAUTILUS** made history. This American submarine travelled under the ice to become the first to reach the waters of the North Pole.

# ANTARCTIC LANDMARKS

## Discover fascinating facts about the geography of the Earth's most extreme continent.

- **ANTARCTICA** is the highest continent, with an average height above sea level of 2500 metres. The land contains many mountain ranges including the Transantarctic Mountains, which run across the whole continent.

- The continent contains just one active volcano: **MOUNT EREBUS**.

- Hidden under Antarctica's ice are over 400 lakes. The largest is called **LAKE VOSTOK** and, with an area of more than 12,500 square kilometres, it's bigger than the Mediterranean island of Cyprus!

- The ceremonial **SOUTH POLE**, near the Amundsen-Scott South Pole Station, is marked by a small, red-and-white-striped pole topped by a chrome globe. It is surrounded by 12 flags, representing the countries that agreed to keep Antarctica clean and free of military forces.

- The **ANTARCTIC PENINSULA** is 1300 kilometres long – that's greater than the distance between London, UK and Madrid, Spain!

Taylor Glacier is home to **BLOOD FALLS**, a waterfall full of chemicals that turn its waters a rusty red colour.

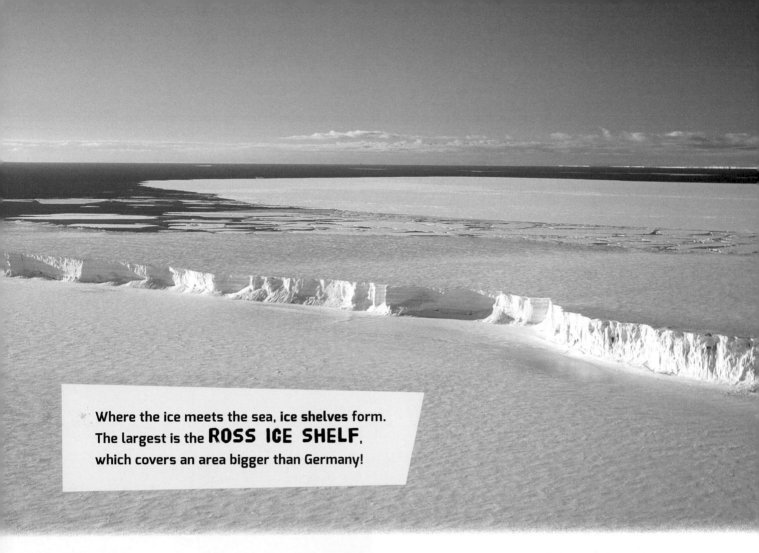

Where the ice meets the sea, ice shelves form. The largest is the **ROSS ICE SHELF**, which covers an area bigger than Germany!

There are seven **CHURCHES** on the continent, built by visitors to Antarctica. These include the 15-metre-tall Trinity Chapel on King George Island.

**CLOSE UP**

## NORTHERN LIGHTS

The incredible light display in this picture occurs above a mountain fjord in Greenland. The northern lights appear in a large region surrounding the magnetic North Pole and are caused by tiny particles streaming out from the Sun. When these particles collide with the Earth's **atmosphere**, a bright light show fills the sky!

## What's in a name?

The scientific term for the light display at the North Pole is *aurora borealis*. It was named by astronomer Galileo Galilei in 1619. *Aurora* is the name of the Ancient Roman goddess of dawn and *Boreas* is the name of the Ancient Greek god of the north wind.

**See what scientists get up to on the planet's chilliest continent!**

# SCIENCE GOES SOUTH

## WEATHER MEASURE

Scientists measure the weather all over Antarctica. Below, they are releasing a weather balloon called a radiosonde, which measures the winds and temperatures in the atmosphere. Some Antarctic winds gust at over 250 kilometres per hour – faster than most cars!

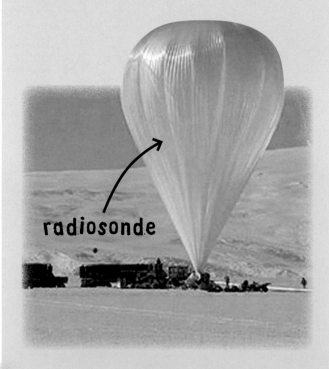

radiosonde

## GOING BACK IN TIME

Ice below the surface of Antarctica was formed many thousands of years ago. Scientists drill cylinders, called ice cores, out of the ice. They analyse what the cores contain to find out what the climate was like in the past. Some of the ice on Antarctica is ancient. In 2006, Japanese scientists recovered an ice core that contained ice thought to be a million years old!

ice core

Scientists use skis and a sled to carry equipment.

## ROCK AND ICE

Scientists discover and study fascinating features found in Antarctica's ice and rock. These include startling ice caves and more than 20,000 meteorites (rocks from space). In 2016, a team on James Ross Island, close to the Antarctic Peninsula, found hundreds of fossils of dinosaurs, which lived around 70 million years ago.

### ice cave

## LIFE ON THE CONTINENT

Some scientists study the wildlife around the coast of the continent. They map populations of seals, penguins and other creatures, measure the wingspans of birds and study their habits. They also dive into the freezing waters to explore the ocean floor, even discovering new species (types of animal) on the way!

chilly!

# INCREDIBLE ICEBERGS

### Your questions about these magnificent chunks of floating ice answered!

## How do icebergs form?

Icy glaciers flow slowly over land in both polar regions. Where they meet the sea, they form an ice shelf with the edge of the ice floating on water. An iceberg occurs when big lumps of ice break off from the ice shelf and drift away in the ocean waters. Scientists call this calving.

## How many icebergs are there?

It's very hard to count them all, but scientists estimate that around 40,000 icebergs are produced in the Arctic Circle alone every year.

## How long do icebergs last?

Some icebergs melt away quickly in weeks or months. Others, though, hang around for years! Most circulate in the polar oceans but a small number travel north from Antarctica or south from the Arctic. In 1926, a small Arctic iceberg was spotted just 210 kilometres off the coast of the island of Bermuda.

## How big are icebergs?

They vary in size from "growlers", which are the size of a car, up to real whoppers! One iceberg spotted in the North Atlantic was 168 metres high – as tall as a 55-storey building. The biggest-ever iceberg was B-15, which broke off the Ross Ice Shelf in Antarctica in 2000. It had an area of around 11,000 square kilometres, bigger than the Caribbean island of Jamaica!

**iceberg in the Arctic Circle**

# POLAR CREATURES

# PENGUIN SPECIES

There are 17 different species of penguin.
Check out 10 of the most fascinating!

## 1 Emperor

This is the tallest and heaviest penguin, standing up to 1.1 metres tall and weighing as much as a typical 12-year-old child! Emperors are the deepest divers, plunging 565 metres below the water's surface. Incredible!

## 2 King

The second largest penguin, king penguins are fussy parents, taking 14–16 months to raise a chick!

## 3 Chinstrap

These penguins love to "toboggan" – skating along the ice on their feathery belly and using their flippers and feet.

## 4 Gentoo

The fastest penguin can race through water four times faster than a human Olympic swimming champion!

## 5 Rockhopper

More punk rock than rockhopper, with their wild spiky head feathers, these small but aggressive birds make their nests on the rocky coasts of islands.

## 6 Yellow-eyed

The world's rarest penguin with just 4000 thought to exist. Found in and around New Zealand, it can live to be 20 years old!

## 7 Adélie

This penguin has a white ring around each eye. It is an excellent swimmer, cruising up to 150 kilometres from its nest.

## 8 Magellanic

These penguins are usually found around South America, but some stray onto the Antarctic coast to hunt for seafood.

## 9 Macaroni

Thought to be the most common penguin with around 18 million in the wild. They are easily spotted due to their orange head feathers.

## 10 Little

This is the smallest penguin species, standing just 33 centimetres tall – it's about the size of a dinner-plate.

# Which penguin is your number one?

# ADAPT TO THE ARCTIC

Many creatures have found ways to survive in the Arctic. Some have special physical adaptations to help them live there.

## WARM COAT

Many Arctic animals are protected from the cold by a thick layer of hair or fur. The musk ox's heavy fur coat is made up of two layers: long, thick guard hairs on the outside and a dense layer of shorter hairs underneath. These layers trap air to warm the musk ox's body while their fur fibres can be spun into *qiviut* wool, which is up to eight times warmer than sheep's wool.

musk ox

## COSY HOME

Little lemmings dig deep, narrow burrows in the snow, often 1–2 metres below the surface. Snow is a good insulator and keeps their burrow temperature warm enough for babies that are born there. The ground squirrel also builds burrows but doesn't stay active in winter. Instead, it goes into **hibernation** – a sort of deep sleep – for months at a time.

lemming

snow geese

## CAMOUFLAGE

The Arctic fox has dark-brown fur in summer. In the autumn, it grows a layer of white fur that makes it hard to spot by potential **prey** as it prowls and hunts in the wintry snow and ice. Arctic hares are also **camouflaged** in white fur, so they can hide from **predators**, such as the fox!

### Arctic fox

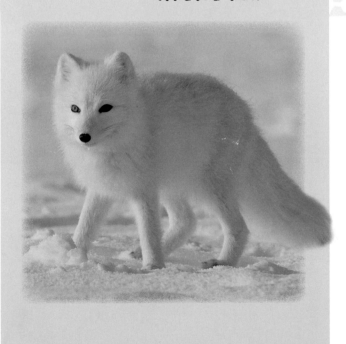

## WINTER BREAK

For some creatures, winter in the Arctic is just too much! They head off on journeys, called **migrations**, to find climates they can tolerate. Caribou herds graze in Alaska's **tundra** in summer, then follow centuries-old trails south to Yukon, Canada, in winter. Snow geese also head south, flying 3000 kilometres in flocks.

### caribou

27

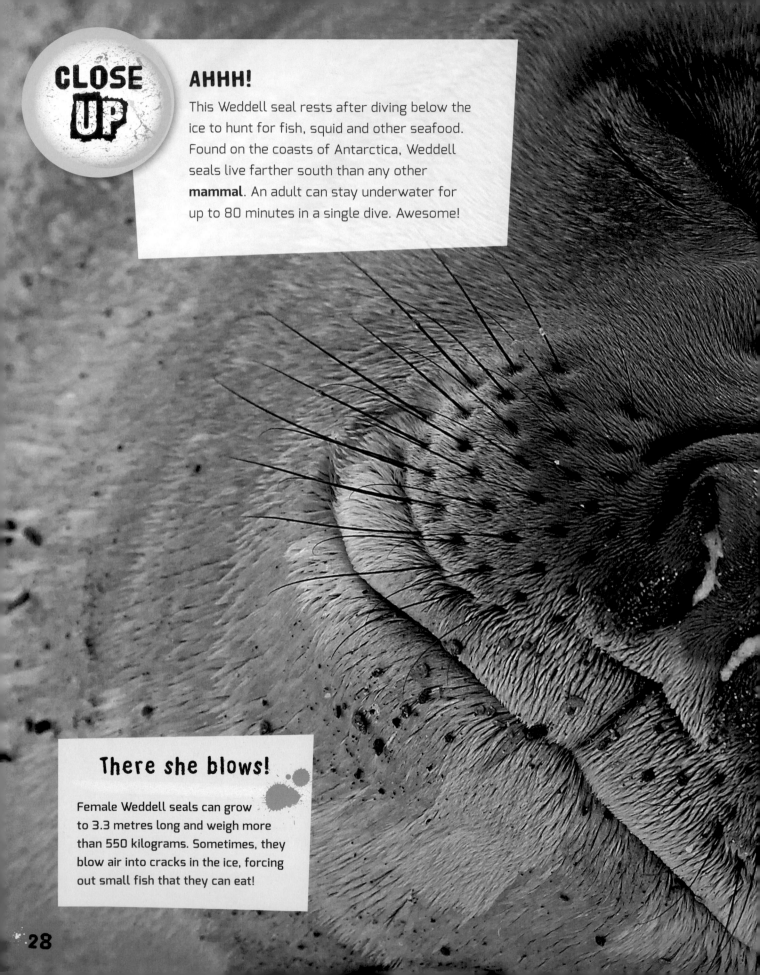

## AHHH!

This Weddell seal rests after diving below the ice to hunt for fish, squid and other seafood. Found on the coasts of Antarctica, Weddell seals live farther south than any other **mammal**. An adult can stay underwater for up to 80 minutes in a single dive. Awesome!

## There she blows!

Female Weddell seals can grow to 3.3 metres long and weigh more than 550 kilograms. Sometimes, they blow air into cracks in the ice, forcing out small fish that they can eat!

29

# POLAR HUNTERS

Want to meet the fiercest predators around the Poles? You've come to the right place!

## 1 Polar bear

Cunning and powerful, the **carnivorous** polar bear stalks the Arctic as the region's top predator. It has keen eyesight and can sniff out the scent of a seal nearly 2 kilometres away. When it strikes, its powerful arms and sharp claws and teeth make quick work of most prey.

## 2 Killer whale (orca)

Found in both Arctic and Antarctic waters, this toothed whale sure has a mean streak. It preys on sharks, seals and even whales!

## 3 Wolverine

These aggressive Arctic animals are just 65–100 centimetres long, but they eat far bigger critters, such as moose!

## 4 Arctic wolf

Wolves attack musk ox, caribou and Arctic hares with their strong jaws that contain 42 sharp teeth!

## 5 Greenland shark

Big (at up to 6.4 metres and 900 kilograms) and beastly, these slow-moving sharks are cold-blooded hunters. They sometimes snap up seals and often feast on fish.

## 6 Walrus

Powerful lip muscles allow a hungry walrus to crack clam shells and suck up what's inside in seconds. An adult walrus might eat as many as 4000 a day!

## 7 Peregrine falcon

A summer visitor to the Arctic, this is the fastest animal on the Earth, flying at over 300 kilometres per hour to catch its prey.

## 8 Leopard seal

These one-tonne terrors lie in wait under an icy ledge. Using powerful jaws, they grab passing penguins – up to six a day!

## 9 Puffins

This Arctic bird can dive to 60 metres underwater. Puffins can store a dozen or more small fish, such as hake, sideways in their big bill.

## 10 Southern elephant seal

The biggest of all seals, these deep-divers plunge over 1 kilometre below sea level to snack on seafood.

# Which polar hunter is your number one?

# BRILLIANT BIRDS

head turner!

Hundreds of different species of bird can be found in the polar regions. They range from tiny Arctic redpolls, which weigh just 15 grams, to powerful imperial shags, which can dive down 50 metres into Antarctic waters to feed.

The **SNOWY OWL** can turn its head three-quarters of the way round. Razor-sharp talons, plus strong eyesight and hearing, make it a lethal foe – especially for lemmings, its favourite food!

FROZEN FACT

stinkers!

**SOUTHERN GIANT PETRELS** pong! They can spit out a foul-smelling oil from their stomach to ward off other creatures. These birds will eat almost anything – including bits of dead seals or whales!

FROZEN FACT

one BIG bird

The **WANDERING ALBATROSS** is the largest flying bird in the world, with a wingspan of up to 3.5 metres. It glides on the wind above the Southern Ocean, cruising 950 kilometres in a day!

**ARCTIC TERNS** leave the Arctic in August and head to Antarctica. They fly back the next June – making migration journeys each year of between 40,000 and 70,000 kilometres.

long-distance champion!

sky pirates

The **SKUA** frequently attacks other birds in mid-air and plunders their food. These scavenger birds think nothing of stealing and eating the eggs or young chicks of other birds.

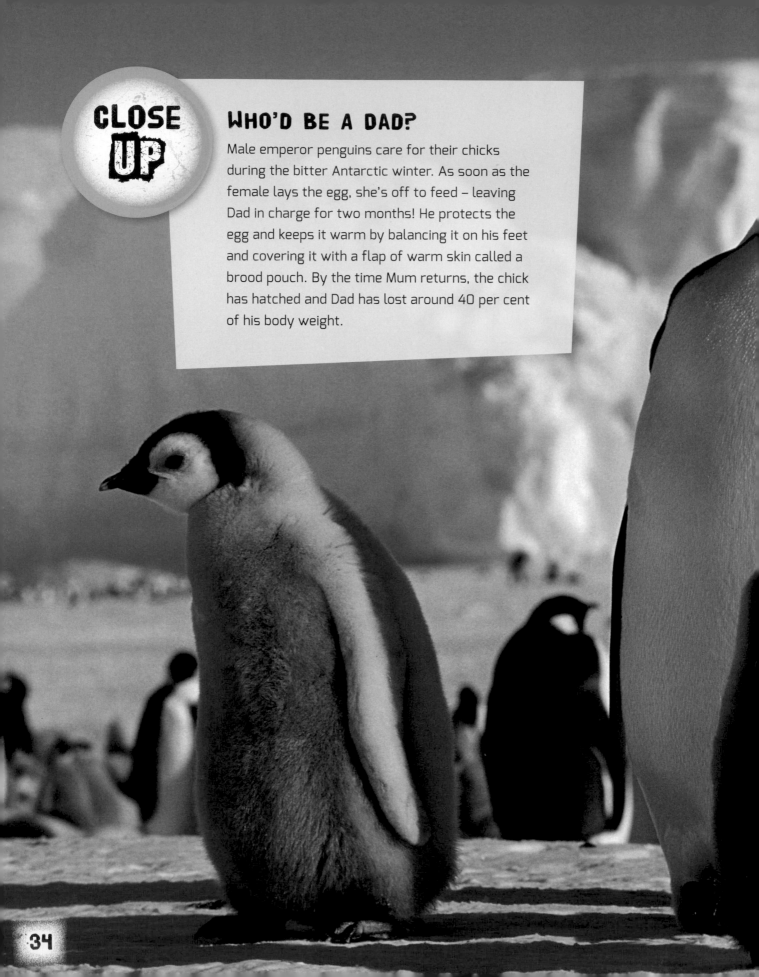

## WHO'D BE A DAD?

Male emperor penguins care for their chicks during the bitter Antarctic winter. As soon as the female lays the egg, she's off to feed – leaving Dad in charge for two months! He protects the egg and keeps it warm by balancing it on his feet and covering it with a flap of warm skin called a brood pouch. By the time Mum returns, the chick has hatched and Dad has lost around 40 per cent of his body weight.

## Chick nursery:

Adult penguins looking after their chicks often huddle together in large colonies to keep warm. Each chick stands on the feet of either its dad or its mum – when she returns – until it is strong enough to cope with the cold Antarctic ice.

# QUESTIONS ABOUT
# POLAR BEARS

Get answers to your questions about the world's biggest hunter on land.

## Polar bears are white, aren't they?

Not really! A polar bear's skin is black, while its outer layer of fur is see-through. Made up of hollow hairs, which measure 5–15 centimetres long, a polar bear's fur reflects the light, making it look white.

## How do polar bears get around?

Polar bears can sprint at 40 kilometres per hour, but only for short distances. The soles of a bear's feet have small bumps and troughs that act like suction cups, keeping them from slipping on the ice. Polar bears are surprisingly good swimmers; they can reach speeds of 10 kilometres per hour mostly using their front legs to paddle.

## How much do they weigh?

An adult male polar bear can weigh over 600 kilograms – that's more than six adult humans! When they are born, it is a different story. A cub is 30–35 centimetres long and weighs around 500 grams – that's about the size of a guinea pig!

## How do polar bears deal with the cold?

Two layers of fur covering a thick layer of body fat, called **blubber**, help **insulate** polar bears from the biting cold weather. A short tail, ears and snout also help by giving off less heat. Sometimes, when winds are especially fierce, polar bears will dig pits in snow banks and curl up into a tight ball inside.

# TOP 10

# PECULIAR POLAR CREATURES

**Presenting the top 10 seriously strange things living in the waters of the polar regions!**

## 1 Lion's mane jellyfish

This GIANT jellyfish has a dome that can grow to 2 metres wide with up to 1200 tentacles, which it uses to sting and capture prey. The tentacles can grow to 33 metres long – that's longer than an NBA basketball court!

## 2 Narwhal

This Arctic Ocean porpoise has a giant tooth, known as a tusk. This tusk grows through its upper lip to a length of 1.5–3.1 metres!

## 7 Hoff crab

This strange creature, found in Antarctica's waters, lets bacteria grow on its chest, then uses comb-like mouthparts to eat them!

## 3 Sea pig

Sea pigs suck up particles from the seabed. Their pink body makes them look like the animals they are named after – pigs!

## 8 Comb jelly

This Arctic jellyfish has rows of moving hairs that push it through the water. The hairs reflect light – making the jelly sparkle!

## 4 Basket star

These strange-looking sea creatures grow tangled masses of arms, all covered in tiny, sharp hooks that help them to catch prey.

## 9 Ice worms

Spending all their lives in glaciers, these worms are so used to the cold that if you warm them up to just 5 degrees Celsius, they turn to liquid!

## 5 Hooded seal

Males of this deep-diving Arctic seal have a balloon-like sac that can be blown up out of one of their nostrils to make sounds that impress the females.

## 10 Arctic lamprey

These funny fish have a sucking mouth with teeth, which they use to attach onto bigger fish and suck out tasty blood to feed on!

## 6 Southern Ocean giant sea spider

Sea spiders in Antarctica are huge. They have eight long, spindly legs, which span up to 35 centimetres.

# Which peculiar creature is your number one?

**SPERM WHALES** have been watched sleeping in the ocean "standing up".

# WHALE OF A TIME!

## Enjoy these facts about the biggest creatures found in the polar oceans!

- The biggest creature on the Earth is the **BLUE WHALE**.

- **KILLER WHALES** (orcas) are really a type of dolphin.

- **BLUE WHALES** feed on tiny, shrimp-like creatures called krill.

- **GREY WHALES** travel 8000–11,000 kilometres across the **Equator** to the Arctic in the summer, then back to the Antarctic when winter looms.

- The biggest brain in the animal kingdom belongs to the **SPERM WHALE**.

A **BLUE WHALE'S** tongue weighs over 2 tonnes and is big enough for an entire football team to stand on.

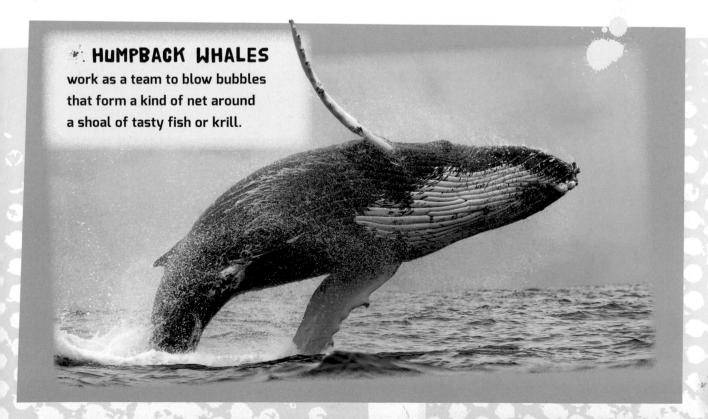

**HUMPBACK WHALES** work as a team to blow bubbles that form a kind of net around a shoal of tasty fish or krill.

# POLAR
# PEOPLE

# ARCTIC PEOPLES

Just over four million people live within the Arctic Circle. Many of them have moved to the Arctic to work in the fishing, oil and gas industries or tourism. Others are descendents of traditional Arctic peoples, who have lived in the region for centuries.

**NENETS** are nomadic reindeer herders. They live in the most northerly parts of Russia and move with the migration of reindeer herds. In the summer, the herds graze deep within the Arctic Circle, then they travel south for the winter.

## Nenets

Greenland

GREENLAND is home to 57,000 people. Its small towns and villages are famous for their brightly coloured houses. People often travel by boat or by dog sled as there aren't many roads.

FROZEN FACT

Found mostly in Alaska, northern Canada and Greenland, the INUIT hunt seals, whales and fish, which they eat cooked or raw. They used to live in tents made of animal skins in summer while in winter, some built igloos out of blocks of snow pressed together.

FROZEN FACT

Inuit

Sami

SAMI people live in parts of Finland, Norway, Sweden and Russia. Their traditional *gákti* dress used to be made from reindeer skin, but today most are made of cotton or wool.

FROZEN FACT

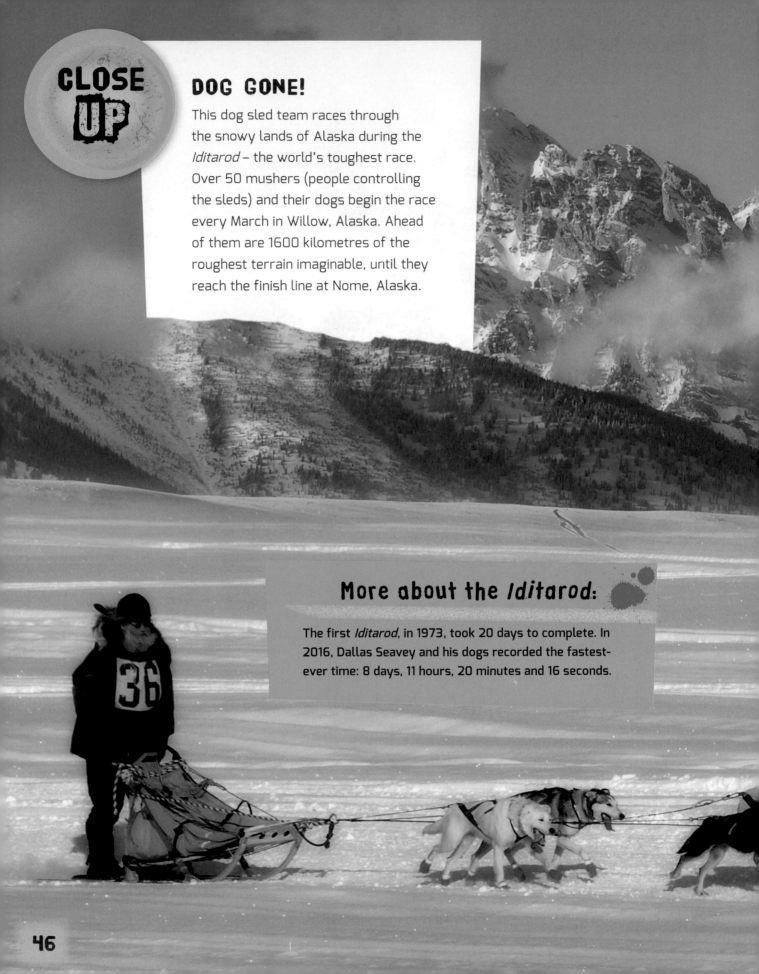

## DOG GONE!

This dog sled team races through the snowy lands of Alaska during the *Iditarod* – the world's toughest race. Over 50 mushers (people controlling the sleds) and their dogs begin the race every March in Willow, Alaska. Ahead of them are 1600 kilometres of the roughest terrain imaginable, until they reach the finish line at Nome, Alaska.

### More about the *Iditarod*:

The first *Iditarod*, in 1973, took 20 days to complete. In 2016, Dallas Seavey and his dogs recorded the fastest-ever time: 8 days, 11 hours, 20 minutes and 16 seconds.

Socks keep their paws warm!

# TOP 10

# POLAR
## EXPLORERS

Check out these
champion explorers
of the Poles.

**1** ### Roald Amundsen

Discoverer of a sea passage between
Greenland and Canada (1903–1906),
this brave Norwegian became the first
person to reach the South Pole (1911).
He was also first to fly over the North
Pole (1926).

## 2 Fridtjof Nansen

The first person to ski across Greenland (1888), this explorer was also first to sail across the whole Arctic Ocean (1893).

## 7 Norman D. Vaughan

Vaughan explored the Antarctic in 1930 with Richard Byrd and, 64 years later, returned to climb Mount Vaughan – a mountain named after him!

## 3 Ranulph Fiennes

This explorer has made over 30 **expeditions** to the polar regions. In 1993, he made the first unsupported walk across Antarctica.

## 8 Edgeworth David

Living off seals and penguins in Antarctica, David (centre) led the first expedition to climb the continent's only active volcano, Mount Erebus.

## 4 Ann Bancroft

Bancroft was the first woman to reach the North Pole on foot and sled (1986) and the first to ski across Antarctica (2001).

## 9 James Clark Ross

This sailor was the first to sail round almost all of the coast of Antarctica (1839–1843), establishing that it is a continent.

## 5 Ernest Shackleton

Shackleton made four expeditions to Antarctica (1901–1922). He explored the Transantarctic mountains and carried out a heroic rescue in 1915–1916.

## 10 David Hempleman-Adams

This explorer gained the first "grand slam": reaching both Poles and climbing the highest mountain on each continent!

## 6 Vivian Fuchs

Fuchs led the first expedition to cross the continent of Antarctica in 1958. The expedition used tractors to cover 3473 kilometres in 99 days.

# Which brave explorer is your number one?

Norwegian team

# RACE TO THE SOUTH POLE

## THE NORWEGIAN EXPEDITION

**TEAM FACTS**

**Leader:** Roald Engelbregt Gravning Amundsen (1872–1928)
**Ship:** *Fram*
**Sailed From:** Kristiania (now called Oslo), Norway
**Arrived in Antarctica:** January 1911
**Base:** Framheim, Bay of Whales

Amundsen set out with four other men and 52 dogs in October 1911. At first they managed to cover 40 kilometres a day, but as the journey grew more difficult, they slowed down. The five had to make their way across a glacier criss-crossed with dozens of cracks and gaps but on 14 December 1911, they planted a Norwegian flag at the South Pole. They returned safely to their base, Framheim, after 99 days and nearly 3000 kilometres of adventuring.

Amundsen made his base 96 kilometres closer to the South Pole than the British team, led by Scott. Amundsen's men were all good skiers and they were equipped with warm fur clothing, similar to that used by Inuit people in the Arctic. Amundsen's team had sleds like those of his rival, Scott, but modified them so they weighed only a quarter of the weight. This meant the Arctic husky dogs needed less effort to pull them.

**amazing Antarctica**

In June 1910, two ships left Europe for the Antarctic. Both carried expeditions led by men intent on being the first to reach the South Pole. The race to be first was on!

Terra Nova team

# THE BRITISH EXPEDITION

**TEAM FACTS**
**Leader:** Robert Falcon Scott (1868–1912)
**Ship:** *Terra Nova*
**Sailed From:** Cardiff, Wales
**Arrived in Antarctica:** January 1911
**Base:** Cape Evans, McMurdo Sound

Robert Falcon Scott hoped to reach the South Pole using ponies, dogs and petrol-powered motor sledges with tracks like a bulldozer. The motor vehicles and ponies turned out to be unsuited to the harsh Antarctic weather and the dog sleds, which started out in November, turned back in December.

Scott pressed on, as one of a party of five who pulled their sleds on foot as they climbed a glacier and reached the South Pole on 17 January 1912, only to discover Amundsen had got there first! They began their 1300-kilometre journey back to safety. It began well, but **blizzards** and temperatures dropping to below minus 40 degrees Celsius slowed their progress. They suffered from frostbite, exhaustion and a shortage of supplies. The team perished in March 1942, just 18 kilometres from a depot full of supplies.

## The Observation Hill cross – a memorial for Scott's team

**1** In 2014, a rock band played a 30-minute gig on an iceberg floating in the Greenland Sea. Rock on!

# TOP 10
# POLAR STUNTS

**Which are the most EXTREME feats staged at the Poles?**

**2**  Lewis Gordon Pugh swam 1000 metres in the icy sea close to the North Pole in 2005 wearing just goggles, a swimhat and his trunks! Double brrr!

**3**  Felicity Aston skied on her own, pulling a sled with a tent and supplies, for 1744 kilometres across Antarctica. Her epic trek took 59 days!

**6** Every November, around 50 extreme athletes trek a 42.2 kilometre-long Antarctic Ice Marathon near the foot of the Ellsworth Mountains.

**7** A number of daredevils have used kites, which catch the fierce polar winds, to kite-ski across part of either the Arctic ice cap or the Antarctic.

**8** Actress and adventurer Manon Ossevoort drove her Massey Ferguson tractor 2500 kilometres to the South Pole in 2014!

**4** Ramon Navarro became the first person to surf in the Antarctic region in 2013 off the coast of the South Shetland Islands. Brrr!

**9** In 2007, TV motoring show presenters Jeremy Clarkson and James May drove to the North Pole in two modified Toyota pick-up trucks.

**5** Maria Leijerstam reached the South Pole on a bicycle! She pedalled 638 kilometres on a bike fitted with skis and 11.3-centimetre-wide balloon tyres.

**10** David Beckham flew to Antarctica in 2015 and played a football match on Union Glacier with staff at the base there. The game ended 3–3.

## BREAKING THE ICE

The Russian icebreaker, NS *Yamal*, crunches through heavy ice in the Arctic Ocean. Icebreakers are strong and sturdy ships that break up ice to let other ships through or to reach and rescue vessels stuck in the ice. Built in 1992, *Yamal* is as long as one and a half football pitches and is powered by two nuclear reactors. This means it can sail for five years before it needs to refuel.

## More about NS Yamal:

The front of the ship, called the prow, is made of extra-thick steel (48 centimetres thick) to withstand impact with the ice. *Yamal*'s sister ship, *Arktika*, was the first ship to muscle through the ice to reach the geographic North Pole in 1977.

Be amazed at these incredible survival stories!

# SURVIVAL

## CAUGHT IN A CREVASSE

**FROZEN FACT**

**Where:** Inland from Commonwealth Bay, Antarctica

**When:** 1912–1913

**Expedition leader:** Douglas Mawson

Mawson

Australian Douglas Mawson was left alone over 250 kilometres from safety after both his team members perished. The first, along with the sled carrying much of their supplies, fell down a deep crack in the ice known as a **crevasse**.

Mawson slowly trekked back through blizzards towards safety when he fell into a crevasse himself. He was dangling in mid-air, from a rope attached to his sled, which was wedged in the crevasse above. Below him was certain death ...

Cold and weak, he pulled himself out of the crevasse's icy jaws and collapsed on the surface. Mawson battled hunger, frostbite and exhaustion yet managed to reach safety at Cape Denison three weeks later.

*"Below was a black chasm. Exhausted, weak and chilled ... I hung with the firm conviction that all was over."*

Douglas Mawson

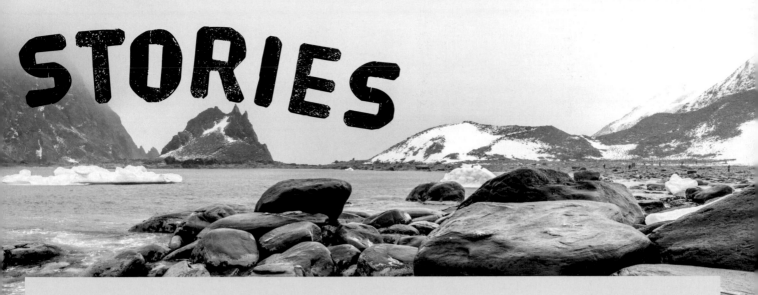

# STORIES

## TRAPPED AND A TREK

**Where:** Weddell Sea to South Georgia
**When:** 1914–1916
**Expedition leader:** Ernest Shackleton

the *Endurance*

Shackleton and his 27-man crew became trapped when their ship, the *Endurance*, got stuck in ice in the Weddell Sea for 10 months. The ship was crushed by the ice and, with no communication or chance of a passing ship, they were in trouble! Shackleton led his crew over the ice, hauling three wooden lifeboats.

Leaving most of the crew on Elephant Island, where they lived off seal meat, Shackleton took five men to sail a lifeboat across over 1200 kilometres of stormy sea to reach South Georgia. The dangerous voyage took 17 days.

Once on South Georgia, Shackleton and two of his crew hiked for 36 hours across glaciers and mountains to find a whaling station on the other side of the island. From there, Shackleton organised rescue attempts, saving the rest of his crew three months later.

*"Our ship crushed and lost and we ourselves drifting on a piece of ice at the mercy of the winds ..."*

Ernest Shackleton

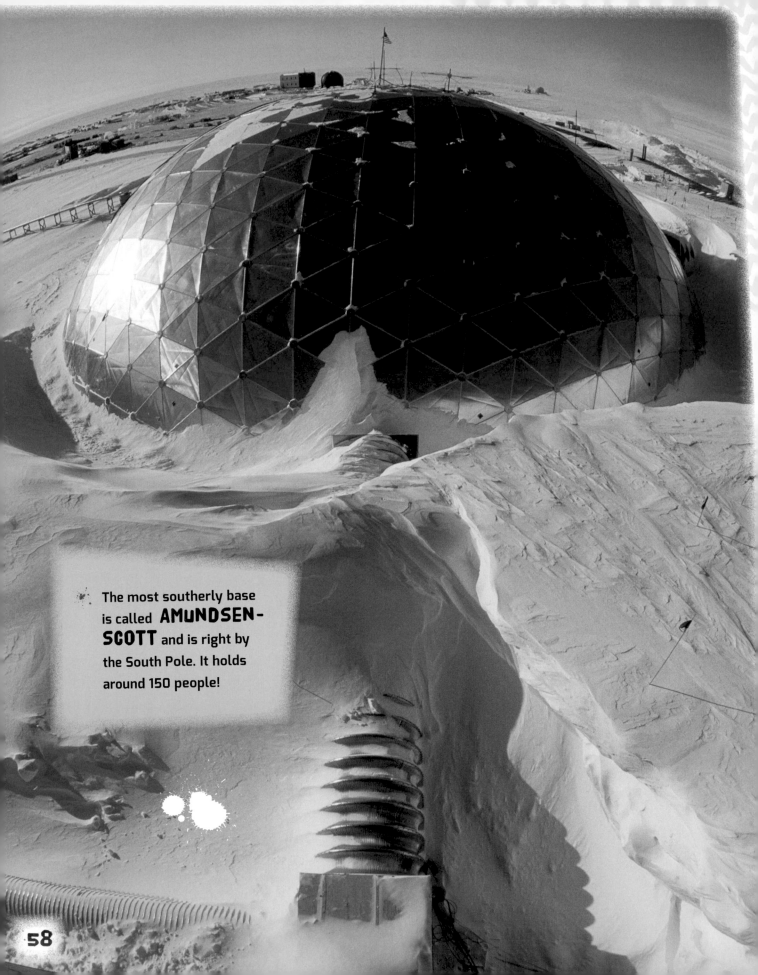

The most southerly base is called **AMUNDSEN-SCOTT** and is right by the South Pole. It holds around 150 people!

# ANTARCTIC BASES

Fuel your fascination with Antarctic stations or bases with these great facts.

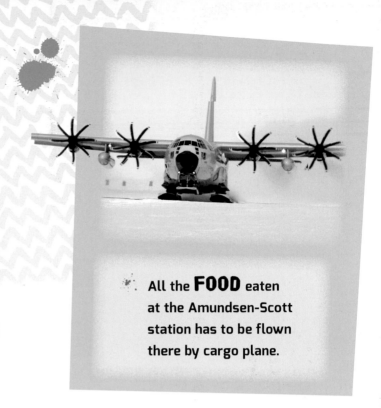

All the **FOOD** eaten at the Amundsen-Scott station has to be flown there by cargo plane.

* There are around **70 PERMANENT BASES** in and around the Antarctic continent.

* The biggest base of all is the USA's **MCMURDO STATION** – it houses up to 1258 people!

* **OPERATION DEEP FREEZE** sees big ships transport around five million kilograms of food and supplies to the McMurdo Station each year.

* **DURING THEIR TIME OFF**, station staff can snap the scenery, go jogging in the snow, ski or even play ice football for exercise.

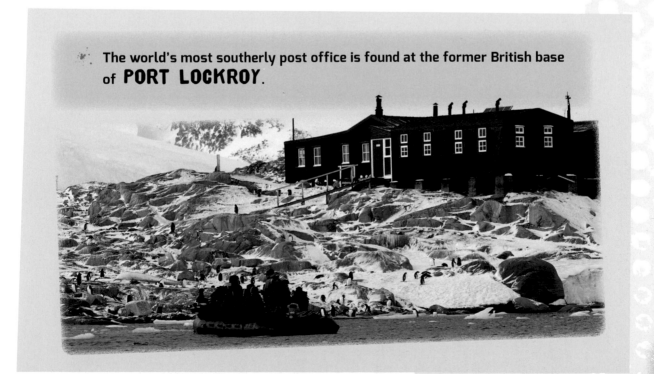

The world's most southerly post office is found at the former British base of **PORT LOCKROY**.

# THE GREAT POLAR QUIZ

Are you an expert on all things polar? Test your knowledge by completing this quiz! When you've answered all of the questions, turn to page 63 to check your score.

 **How many people live in Antarctica permanently**
a) 0
b) 500
c) 50,000

 **Can you name the largest ice shelf in Antarctica?**
a) Larsen Ice Shelf
b) Nansen Ice Shelf
c) Ross Ice Shelf

 **Who reached the North Pole by dogsled in 1986?**
a) Will Smith
b) Will Steger
c) Willy Wonka

 **How many tourists visit Antarctica each year?**
a) 5000
b) 40,000
c) 350,000

 **How many meteorites have been found in Antarctica?**
a) 18
b) 450
c) Over 20,000

 **How big are growler icebergs?**
a) the size of a car
b) the size of a house
c) the size of a jumbo jet

 **How many icebergs do scientists think are produced in the Arctic Circle each year?**
a) 8000
b) 40,000
c) 2,000,000

 **The cerimonial South Pole is marked by what?**
a) a blue igloo
b) a red-and-white-striped pole
c) a star-shaped flag

 **Which creature turns to liquid if you heat it to 5 degrees Celsius?**
a) Ice snail
b) Ice snake
c) Ice worm

**How much does a baby polar bear weigh at birth?**
a) 7 grams
b) 40 grams
c) 500 grams

 **Which creature can eat around 1600 lemmings a year?**
a) Greenland shark
b) Polar bear
c) Snowy owl

 **Which flying visitor to the Arctic can dive at speeds of over 300 kilometres per hour?**
a) Arctic tern
b) Peregrine falcon
c) Snow goose

 **What is the biggest creature on the Earth?**
a) Beluga whale
b) Blue whale
c) Minke whale

 **How long can the tentacles of a lion's mane jellyfish grow to?**
a) 33 centimetres
b) 3.3 metres
c) 33 metres

 **Which Arctic mammal's thick coat produces *qiviut* wool?**
a) Caribou
b) Musk ox
c) Yak

 **How many clams can an adult walrus eat in a day?**
a) 100
b) 800
c) 4000

 **How much does a Weddell seal weigh?**
a) More than 50 kilograms
b) More than 500 kilograms
c) More than 550 kilograms

 **Which is the biggest and heaviest penguin species?**
a) Emperor
b) King
c) Gentoo

**What is the name of the largest scientific base on Antarctica?**
a) McMurdo Station
b) Port Lockroy
c) Scott-Amundsen South Pole Station

 **In what year did Roald Amundsen reach the South Pole?**
a) 1909
b) 1911
c) 1913

 **How long can a narwhal's tusk grow to?**
a) 80 centimetres
b) 1.5 metres
c) 3.1 metres

# GLOSSARY

**Arctic Circle**
An imaginary line around the northernmost part of the Earth. The land and sea above this line is known as the Arctic.

**atmosphere**
The gases that surround the Earth.

**blizzard**
A heavy snowstorm, which comes with high winds.

**blubber**
A thick layer of fat under the skin, which helps keep animals warm.

**camouflage**
Colours and patterns that blend in with a creature's surroundings making the creature hard to see.

**carnivorous**
A meat-eating creature, such as a polar bear, a seal or a shark.

**continent**
One of the seven large land masses found on the Earth: Africa, Antarctica, Oceania, Asia, Europe, North America and South America.

**crevasse**
A deep, usually vertical, crack or split in a glacier.

**equator**
An imaginary line around the middle of the Earth, which marks the mid-point between the North Pole and South Pole.

**expedition**
A journey made by a group of people with a particular aim, such as exploring unmapped lands or performing scientific work.

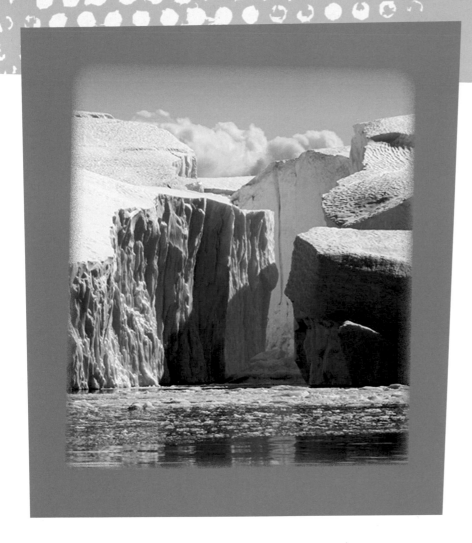

### glacier
A mass of icy land that flows downhill slowly.

### hibernation
A deep, sleep-like state that some animals enter through a winter.

### iceberg
A large piece of floating ice that has calved, or broken off, a glacier or ice shelf.

### ice shelf
A large amount of ice that is attached to land, but extends out into the sea or ocean.

### insulate
To surround or cover something to help stop heat loss.

### krill
Tiny, shrimp-like creatures, which live in huge numbers in seas and oceans.

### mammal
A warm-blooded animal that feeds its young on milk.

### migration
A long journey some animals make each year to a distant place, often to feed and breed, followed by a return trip back.

### nomadic
To constantly move homes instead of living in just one place. People who follow animal migrations are nomadic.

### peninsula
A peninsula is an area of land that juts out into the sea and has water on three of its sides.

### polar
To do with the regions of the North Pole and or South Pole of the planet.

### predator
A creature that hunts other creatures for food.

### prey
A creature that is hunted for food by other creatures.

### tundra
An area where few trees or plants grow due to extremely cold weather and short growing seasons.

QUIZ ANSWERS: 1 = a, 2 = c, 3 = b, 4 = b, 5 = c, 6 = a, 7 = b, 8 = b, 9 = c, 10 = c, 11 = c, 12 = b, 13 = b, 14 = c, 15 = b, 16 = c, 17 = c, 18 = a, 19 = a, 20 = b, 21 = c.

# INDEX

## A
Alaska 27, 45, 46
albatrosses 33
Amundsen, Roald 13, 48, 50
Antarctica 6, 11, 14–19, 49, 58–59
Arctic 10
Arctic Circle 10, 20, 44
Arctic foxes 27
Arctic hares 27, 31
Arctic Ocean 6, 10, 49
Arctic terns 33
Arctic wolves 31
*Aurora Borealis* 16–17

## B
Bancroft, Ann 49
bases and science stations 11, 19, 58–59
Beckham, David 53

## C
caribou 27, 31
churches 15
crabs 39
crevasses 56

## D, E, F
David, Edgeworth 49
dinosaurs 19
dog sleds 45, 46–47, 50, 51
emperor penguins 24, 34–35
explorers 13, 48–51
Fiennes, Ranulph 49
fish 39, 45
Fuchs, Vivian 49

## G, H
glaciers 14, 20, 53
Greenland 16, 45
ground squirrels 26
Hempleman-Adams, David 49

## I
ice caves 19
ice cores 18
ice shelves 15, 20, 21
icebergs 20–21, 52
   calving 20
   growlers 21
icebreakers (ships) 54–55
*Iditarod* (dog sled race) 46–47
Inuit 13, 45, 50

## J, K, L
jellyfish 38, 39
killer whales (orcas) 31, 41
lakes 14
lemmings 26, 32

## M
Mawson, Douglas 56
meteorites 19
mountains 10, 11, 14, 49
musk oxen 26, 31

## N
Nansen, Fridtjof 49
narwhals 39
Nenets 44
nomads 10, 44
North Pole 6, 10, 12–13, 48, 49, 53, 55
   magnetic North Pole 12, 16
Northern Lights 16–17

## P
Peary, Robert 13
penguins 11, 24–25, 31, 34–35
people 10, 11, 13, 42–59
peregrine falcons 31
petrels 32
polar bears 30, 36–37
polar stunts 52–53
puffins 31

## R
reindeer 10, 44, 45
Ross, James Clark 49
Ross Ice Shelf 15, 21

## S
Sami people 45
Scott, Robert Falcon 51
seals 28–29, 31, 39, 45
settlements 10, 11
Shackleton, Ernest 49, 57
sharks 31
skuas 33
snow geese 27
snowy owls 32
South Pole 6, 11, 14, 48, 50–51, 53, 58
Southern Ocean 11
spiders 39
survival stories 56–57

## T, V
temperatures 10, 11
tourism 11, 44
tundra 27
Vaughan, Norman D. 49
volcanoes 14, 49

## W
walruses 31
waterfalls 14
weather balloons 18
whales 31, 40–41, 45
wildlife 22–41
   adaptations 26–27
   birds 24–25, 27, 31, 32–35
   camouflage 27
   migrations 27, 44
   ocean 38–41
   predators 27, 30–31
winds 18
wolverines 31